My Name is Isabella

A Collection of Stories about People who Share my Name

By Allison Dearstyne

"[I was proud] to show just what a woman can do when the chance comes her way."   - Isabella Goodwin

Dedicated to every girl named Isabella. When the chance comes your way, do wonderful things!

The name Isabella originally came from the name Elizabeth. The name Elizabeth came from the Hebrew name Elisheba several thousand years ago. Speakers of a language called Occitan translated the name Elizabeth to Elisabel, which became Isabel. In French, the name Isabel is translated Isabelle, in Scottish it's translated Isobel and in Italian it's translated Isabella. The name Isabella means "Pledged to God."

There have been many great women through history who have shared your name! In this book, we will look at the lives of these seven remarkable women named Isabella:

Isabella Baumfree
Isabella Bird
Isabella Pringle
Isabella Beecher Hooker
Isabella Karle
Isabella Whitney
Isabella Goodwin

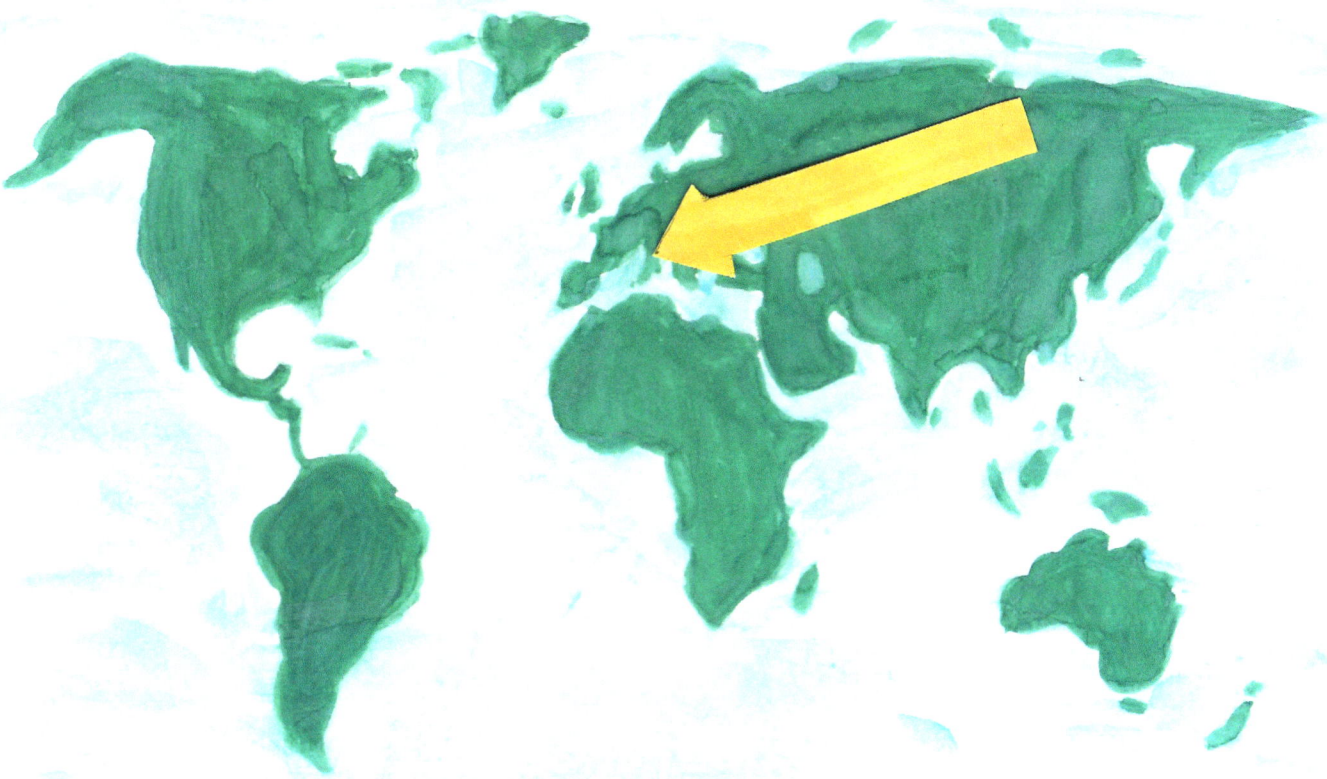

Isabella Baumfree was a Black American evangelist, abolitionist, women's rights activist and author best known by her pen name, Sojourner Truth. She was born a slave in 1797 in New York and suffered greatly through her early years. Throughout her childhood and teenage years, she was bought and sold four times to cruel masters. She married another slave named Thomas and together they had five children.

Isabella Baumfree's last master promised her that he would grant her freedom on July 4, 1826, if she was a hardworking slave for him. She held up her end of the bargain but when the date arrived, her master changed his mind and wouldn't release her. Furious, she walked away from him as quickly as she could, clutching her baby girl in her arms. Later Isabella Baumfree explained that she didn't run because she believed that would be wicked, but instead she walked off, knowing she was in the right.

Tragically, she had to leave her other children behind because they were still legally bound to her master. Isabella Baumfree and her baby were taken in by a Christian abolitionist couple, Isaac and Maria Van Wagenen. Abolitionists worked to end slavery. While she was living with them, Isabella Baumfree's master found her and tried to reclaim her. In response, the Van Wagenens bought her freedom. The next year in 1827, a law passed in New York that freed all slaves in the state.

But Isabella Baumfree's troubles were far from over. Illegally, her former master sold her five-year-old son to slave owners in Alabama. The Van Wagenens helped her file a lawsuit to get him back. After several months, she won her case and regained custody of her son. In doing so, she became the first Black woman to sue a White man in the United States and win!

Moved by the kindness of the Van Wagenens, Isabella Baumfree became a Christian with a fervor that grew for the rest of her life. She earned a living as a housekeeper for several preachers, and she became a bolder witness for her faith. In 1843 she renamed herself Sojourner Truth, believing she had a religious obligation to go forth, preach the gospel and speak out against slavery.

Sojourner Truth spoke these wise words: "Children, who made your skin White? Was it not God? Who made mine Black? Was it not the same God?"

On her campaign to speak the truth, Sojourner Truth met several people who greatly influenced her and vice versa. She became friends with Frederick Douglass, Susan B. Anthony, Abraham Lincoln and many others. Everywhere she went, she commanded attention. She stood six feet tall and had huge muscles from years of manual labor.

Throughout the American Civil War, she supported the Union by recruiting soldiers and organizing supplies for Black troops. After the Union won the Civil War, she helped newly freed slaves find jobs. As an old lady, she lived with her daughters in Michigan, where she wrote her autobiography, *The Narrative of Sojourner Truth.* A friend helped her by writing down the words as she spoke, since she had never learned to read or write.

Despite her lack of formal education, Sojourner Truth was a powerful speaker and author. Her most famous speech is called "Ain't I a Woman?" and it argues for rights of both women and Black people. She was a champion for human rights her entire life.

Sojourner Truth was a great American hero! She used her troubled early life as a slave to help others. Think of ways you can use your experiences to help others too, and you can be like strong Isabella Baumfree!

Isabella Bird was a British explorer, writer and photographer. She was born in 1831 in Yorkshire. As a little girl she was frail, suffering from back pain, headaches and insomnia. In 1850, she had a tumor removed from her spine, and her health continued to decline. Her doctor encouraged her to travel overseas to improve her health.

So, when an opportunity arose for Isabella Bird to sail to the United States and stay with relatives, she jumped at the chance. There, she wrote and published her first book, *An Englishwoman in America*, describing her experiences. Isabella Bird continued her writing and her travels, first to Australia, then to Hawaii, where she climbed several mountains despite her poor health. Then she heard that the mountains and air in Colorado were good for the sickly, so she moved there. Colorado had not yet become a state, and it was filled with rattlesnakes, outlaws and danger.

In a letter to her sister, she wrote, "This is no region for tourists and women, only for a few elk and bear hunters at times, and its unprofaned freshness gives me new life."

On horseback she rode over 800 miles through the Rocky Mountains. She insisted on riding horses safely - frontwards like a man, not sidesaddle, which was the only acceptable way for a woman to ride a horse in those days. During her time in Colorado, she wrote her most famous book, *A Lady's Life in the Rocky Mountains*. When her book became an international bestseller, suddenly people all over wanted to visit Estes Park! Today, rangers at Rocky Mountain National Park call Isabella Bird the mother of the region.

She captivated several outlaws on her adventures who loved her independent mind, ability to live outdoors and fearlessness. Seasoned ranchers declared Isabella Bird a better cattle driver than a man. Dressed in cumbersome women's clothing and without any technical equipment she climbed Colorado's highest mountains with her pals, unruly mountain men who fell in love with her.

But the man she eventually married wasn't a mountain man or an outlaw, but a Scottish surgeon. Doctor John Bishop, who prescribed her travels in the first place, proposed to her and she waited to accept until she had traveled some more. After spending time in Japan, China, Korea, Vietnam and Singapore, she decided to marry him. Their marriage was both happy and tragically short. He only lived five more years and she suffered from scarlet fever. But she recovered, determined to keep going.

Isabella Bird studied medicine and became a missionary. She funded and helped build a hospital for women in India. Through her travels, writing and photographs, she became famous. Wherever she went, she interviewed local people and wrote about their different customs. Isabella Bird established hospitals and schools in many countries she visited. When she was 70, she took her last journey to Morocco, where the Sultan gave her a stallion that she rode proudly.

Isabella Bird led a big life! When you travel to a new place, write about your experiences - the geography, the people you meet and your adventures. Then you can be like extraordinary Isabella Bird!

Isabella Beecher Hooker was an American activist and suffragist. She was born in 1822 in Connecticut, the fifth of 13 children born to the famous Reverend Lyman Beecher. She, like many of her siblings, became a fearless leader.

She married John Hooker, a young lawyer and abolitionist. He influenced Isabella, helping her to see the importance of ending slavery. Together they had three children, and she spent many years focusing her efforts on the important work of raising them and trying to end slavery. When the American Civil War ended, slavery finally became illegal.

Then Isabella Beecher Hooker turned her energies toward the women's movement, specifically for suffrage, or the right to vote. She helped found the New England Women Suffrage Association. With the legal aid of her husband, she wrote and presented a bill to the Connecticut General Assembly that gave married women property rights. The bill was rejected, but Isabella Beecher Hooker didn't give up! She reintroduced the bill every year until it finally passed in 1877.

She became friends with other suffragists like Susan B. Anthony and Elizabeth Cady Stanton. Together they worked tirelessly to convince Congress to give women the right to vote. Finally in 1920, 13 years after Isabella Beecher Hooker's death, women were given the right to vote in the United States.

It was a long and hard road for women to win the right to vote. One day you will be old enough to vote. When you go to the polls, be thankful for people like Isabella Beecher Hooker, who made voting possible for you!

Isabella Pringle was a Scottish doctor and pioneer in child health. She was born in Edinburgh in 1876. As a young woman she worked as a secretary, but she dreamed of something more. When she was 29, she decided to study medicine at the University of Edinburgh and graduated four years later.

While working at a hospital, Isabella Pringle realized a great need in Scotland: Children and pregnant women did not get the proper care they needed. She also realized that she needed to continue her education to best meet their needs. So, she earned her M.D., which led to her promotion to oversee the maternity and child program where she worked. She was the first woman to hold the position of senior assistant medical officer.

It took 20 years for Isabella Pringle to build complete service programs for her patients. Under her leadership, these programs thrived and paved the way for Scotland's National Health Service, which officially began decades later. Isabella Pringle was the first woman to become a Fellow of the Royal College of Physicians of Edinburgh in 1929.

Because she was the first woman to do so many things, we call Isabella Pringle a pioneer! At your next visit to your pediatrician, think about Isabella Pringle, who worked hard to provide great medical care for kids like you!

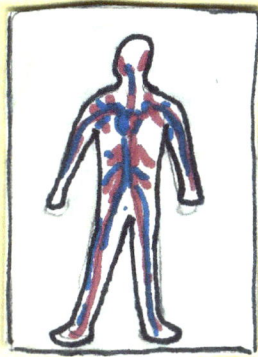

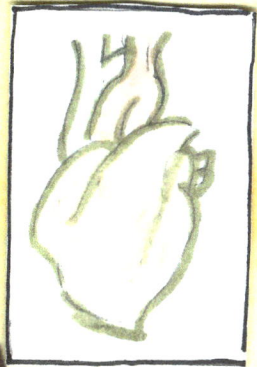

Isabella Karle was a world-famous scientist who specialized in crystallography. She was born in 1921 in Detroit, the daughter of Polish immigrants. As a little girl, she loved science and was inspired by reading a biography of physicist Marie Curie. When she was in high school, she had a female chemistry teacher who encouraged her to pursue her dream to become a chemist. Another teacher told her that chemistry was not a proper field for girls. Both teachers provided motivation in her journey to become a scientist.

She attended the University of Michigan, where she earned her Ph.D. While in school, she went to a lab where she was seated alphabetically next to Jerome Karle. Sparks flew in the lab, and the two married in 1942. Together they worked on the Manhattan Project, helping build the two atomic bombs that were dropped on Japan, ending World War II. Afterward, she joined her husband working at the Naval Research Laboratory in Washington state.

Specifically, the Karles worked together to improve x-ray crystallography, which is a tool used for determining the atomic structure of crystals. Before their work, the process was time-consuming and difficult. The Karles' direct method solved these problems. Their method led to the study of thousands of molecules every year. Among those molecules were toxins, drugs to treat bacterial infections, explosives, cancer-fighting molecules and much more. Their method has affected your life in many ways!

In 1985, Jerome Karle was awarded the Nobel Prize in Chemistry with mathematician Herbert Hauptman. Many scientists believed that Isabella Karle should have shared the prize, and no one fought for her proper recognition harder than her husband. Although she was never awarded a Nobel Prize, she won several honors in her later years. The Karles enjoyed a long and happy marriage. Together they had three daughters who all became scientists too.

Isabella Karle made contributions that changed the world! When you are in your science class, pay close attention and you can be like smart Isabella Karle!

Isabella Whitney was the first professional woman writer in England. She born around 1546 into a middle-class family in Cheshire. When she was a young woman, she moved to London to work as a maid. While living there she wrote poems about her experiences in the city she grew to love. Then for unknown reasons, she lost her job and moved back home with her parents. Here's an excerpt from one of her poems about leaving London:

> The time is come, I must depart from thee, ah famous city;
> I never yet to rue my smart, did find that thou had'st pity.

To earn money for her family she sold her poems to be published. Women in Isabella Whitney's society were snubbed for doing "men's work" like writing and earning income for it. Sending out her poems to be published was very bold. Isabella Whitney's most famous work was an advice-giving volume of poems called *A Sweet Nosegay.*

Her poems were known for being forward-thinking. She criticized gender roles that made women powerless. Women were expected to remain under the control of their fathers and husbands, and Isabella Whitney did the opposite of this. Some people believed that these ideas were dangerous.

Isabella Whitney used witty humor to talk about politics, social class and wealth. During her time, most writers published books about Christian topics. Isabella Whitney's poems stood out for being secular, or non-religious. People in both the upper and middle class enjoyed her work.

It has been said that well-behaved women rarely made history. Isabella Whitney was one such woman. Try writing a poem and you can be like witty Isabella Whitney!

Isabella Goodwin was New York City's first female police detective. She was born in Manhattan in 1865, married a policeman when she was 19 and had four children. Her husband died young, leaving her to support her family alone.

She passed a civil service exam and was hired by future President Theodore Roosevelt to be a police matron. She worked long hours looking after women prisoners for little pay while her mother watched her children. In the meantime, Isabella Goodwin gained a reputation in the police department for her skill at going undercover to expose crooks. She approached fortune tellers and fake healers pretending to be naïve and then busted them when they tried to swindle her.

Isabella Goodwin made her big break in 1912. In the middle of the day $25,000 was stolen from a bank in Manhattan, and the bandits got away! There were 60 detectives hired who could not crack the case. The story was all over the news. It was a huge embarrassment for the New York Police Department.

Then a rumor surfaced when a shopkeeper gave a clue needed to identify the number one suspect: a gangster named Eddie Kinsman and his girlfriend "Swede Annie" Hull were suddenly spending huge amounts of money. So, Isabella Goodwin went undercover as a maid at a boardinghouse where Swede Annie lived. Putting on ragged clothes and a fake Irish accent, Isabella Goodwin listened at keyholes between scrubbing floors and chatted up Swede Annie to get a confession. With her stellar snooping skills, she uncovered enough evidence for police to arrest Eddie Kinsman.

The morning after the arrest, Isabella Goodwin was promoted to the rank of detective lieutenant, becoming the first woman to hold the position. A few years later, she oversaw 26 female officers. Throughout her career, she helped secure many high-profile arrests. Isabella Goodwin believed that women made good detectives because of their natural intuition. She said that she could sense things even when she didn't have proof.

Isabella Goodwin was clever and plucky. It would make her proud to know how many women work as police officers and detectives today. One day, you will join the work force too. When you do, be thankful for women like Isabella Goodwin, who helped pave the way for you!

This page is all about you!

_____ was born on

_____

As a baby, Isabella _____

_____

As a little girl, Isabella _____

_____

Isabella is especially good at _____

_____

Isabella is often described as _____

_____

Isabella makes people laugh when she _____

_____

One day Isabella would like to _____

_____

This page is for making a self-portrait. A self-portrait is a picture of you, drawn by you!

Bibliography

"Dr. Isabella Pringle (1876-1963)." *ed.ac.uk.* The University of Edinburgh. 25 Sept. 2017. Web. 14 Apr. 2019.

Encyclopaedia Britannica Editors. "Isabella Beecher Hooker." *Encyclopaedia Britannica, inc.* Encyclopaedia Britannica. 18 Feb. 2019. Web. 11 Apr. 2019.

History.com Editors. "Sojourner Truth." History. *A&E Television Networks.* 02 Nov. 2018. Web. 28 Mar. 2019.

"Isabella Whitney." *poetryfoundation.org.* Poetry foundation. Web. 28 Jul. 2022

Kilgannon, Corey. "Overlooked No More: Isabella Goodwin, New York City's First Female Police Detective." *nytimes.com.* The New York Times. 13 Mar. 2019. Web. 26 Oct. 2023.

Langer, Emily. "Isabella Karle: Chemist who revealed molecular structures and helped husband win Nobel prize." *independent.co.uk.* Independent. 15. Nov. 2017. Web. 09 May 2019.

Levins, Sandy. "Isabella Goodwin : NYPD's First Female Police Detective." *wednesdayswomen.com.* Wednesday's Women. 25 Dec. 2019. Web. 26 Oct 2023.

Michals, Debra. "Sojourner Truth." *womenshistory.org.* National Women's History Museum. Web. 31 Mar. 2019.

Ross, Tracy. "Seven Reasons Isabella Bird Should be Your New Role Model." *visitestespark.com.* Rocky Mountain National Park. 04 Jan. 2019. Web. 03 Apr. 2019.

Wang, Linda. "Isabella Karle dies at age 95." *cen.acs.org* Chemical & Engineering News. 26 Oct. 2017. Web. 08 May 2019.

Wikipedia contributors. "Isabella (given name)." *Wikipedia, The Free Encyclopedia.* Wikipedia, The Free Encyclopedia, 4 Apr. 2019. Web. 9 May. 2019.

Wikipedia contributors. "Isabella Bird." *Wikipedia, The Free Encyclopedia.* Wikipedia, The Free Encyclopedia, 27 Mar. 2019. Web. 3 Apr. 2019.

Wikipedia contributors. "Isabella Beecher Hooker." *Wikipedia, The Free Encyclopedia.* Wikipedia, The Free Encyclopedia, 1 Mar. 2019. Web. 12 Apr. 2019.

Wikipedia contributors. "Isabella Pringle." *Wikipedia, The Free Encyclopedia.* Wikipedia, The Free Encyclopedia, 11 Jun. 2018. Web. 15 Apr. 2019.

Wikipedia contributors. "Isabella Whitney." *Wikipedia, The Free Encyclopedia.* Wikipedia, The Free Encyclopedia, 3 Nov. 2021. Web. 28 Jul. 2022.

www.ingramcontent.com/pod-product-compliance
Lightning Source LLC
Chambersburg PA
CBHW042110040426
42448CB00002B/218